I Will

Poetry for the Soul

DR. CHERYL GREEN

WESTBOW
PRESS®
A DIVISION OF THOMAS NELSON
& ZONDERVAN

WestBow Press books may be ordered through booksellers or by contacting:

WestBow Press
A Division of Thomas Nelson & Zondervan
1663 Liberty Drive
Bloomington, IN 47403
www.westbowpress.com
1 (866) 928-1240

Because of the dynamic nature of the Internet, any web addresses or
links contained in this book may have changed since publication and may
no longer be valid. The views expressed in this work are solely those
of the author and do not necessarily reflect the views of the publisher,
and the publisher hereby disclaims any responsibility for them.

Any people depicted in stock imagery provided by Thinkstock are models,
and such images are being used for illustrative purposes only.
Certain stock imagery © Thinkstock.

ISBN: 978-1-5127-8038-3 (sc)
ISBN: 978-1-5127-8037-6 (e)

Library of Congress Control Number: 2017904410

Print information available on the last page.

WestBow Press rev. date: 05/17/2017

Reviews

In the words of Frenchman Joseph Roux: *Poetry is truth in Sunday clothes*- a perfect quote to describe this collection of poetry. Cheryl has captured the ability to integrate principals from the greatest and oldest book in the world in a way that is relevant and modern. It forces a connection with your whole being-mind, body and spirit. Reading so immerses you, you feel the illusion of having the experience without actually going through the emotions. An absolute must read for everyone who understands the love of God, the favor & grace he provides and the pull of the world.

-Dr. Seun Ross, DNP, MSN, RN, CRNP-F, NP-C, NEA-BC
Director of Nursing Practice and Work Environment American Nurses Association
President Chi Zeta Chapter, Sigma Theta Tau International Honor Society

A book of poems that reflects the message of the soul. In this book of poems Dr. Green used a variety of topics, themes and concepts to express conflicts, turmoil, and emotions from within. Dr. Green's rich and lavish use of metaphors and similes, creates meaning and a sense of life and purpose to each poem.

A great read for reflection, hope and courage.

-Dr. Vivienne Friday, PhD, RN
Associate Director Bridgeport Hospital School of Nursing

Cheryl's majestic body of poems reflect her articulation of praise to God, which is reflective of her affinity to acceptance and not excluding other various religions. I appreciate the flow and scripting of numerous diverse poems. Cheryl, delivers what I'll frame as a quiet storm theme in her writing. I sense that she is not on a soap box or raising her voice for effect, but affording you some insight into her affinities and thoughts.

Harry L. Green, B.S., MBA
Corporate Executive-Retiree
Working Artist Oil Painting

Cheryl's poems "Poetry for the Soul" are extraordinary, poignant and weave evocative stories of life struggles. The poems takes one through many tumultuous times with issues of abuse, grief, loss of friends and family, betrayal and ultimately God's healing and forgiveness. I was especially moved by the peoms titled "Judas" that says "all of us have a Judas within us", and "She" - following her breast removal, the woman and her husband pray together and "she," believes in her healing, is no longer afraid and feels a sense of peace.

Merlyn V. LaPaix, MSN, MBA
Retired Director of Nursing, Yale New Haven Hospital

Foreword

This collection of forty three short poems, prayers, and reflections covers a wide range of experiences that shape our lives. From strong words about betrayal in "Judas" and "Whispers" to the quiet sentiment in "Lullaby for a Child", Dr. Green expresses the wide range of emotional and spiritual realities within us.

"Broken" and "Johnny" tell stories of suffering imposed upon us while "Toxicity" speaks of the suffering we cause others. Yet "Heard" and "Invited" resonate with hope that our pain, failures, and brokenness are met by the love of God. "Bloom" is hopeful that life will be full, while "Rush" is frustrated with the seemingly unceasing demands that leave us thinking "I need to slow down, but when?"

There are two main elements I especially appreciate in this collection.

One is how these poems, like the Book of Psalms, move freely back and forth in regards to our emotional and spiritual condition. Just as our mood and attitudes can fluctuate within minutes, the author places "Invited," which invites us to dwell with God, just before "Gone" which describes the emptiness of life at the loss of someone we love.

The second element I appreciated is the simplicity of language and form of all the poems. Only a couple of the poems are more than one page and the words and forms used are direct, clear and evocative. The language provides direct access to the emotional realities highlighted by the poem so that the reader is not left to intellectualize about what a word or image might mean but is rather left to address the emotions stirred by the force of the poem.

Overall, these poems have a spiritual tone shaped by Christian faith, but the author does not minimize the loss, suffering and confusion that impact people of faith as well as everyone else. Instead, she gives powerful and simple words to difficult feelings and experiences others of us may not know how to express. One of the final poems catches the sentiment I sensed throughout the collection when she prays, with hope that God will, "Find me in my horrid mess."

Once again, like the Psalms, some of the poems in this collection will not speak to you right at the moment, but others will do so deeply and eventually they all do since we all share the realities expressed in these poems. Whether or not you share the author's Christian faith, this collection could serve as a rich resource of reflection, meditation and prayer.

Reverend William Cutler
InterVarsity Christian Fellowship Graduate and Faculty Ministries
Yale University Medical School
Southern Connecticut State University

Contents

Thank You

I will obey you in spite of my brokenness because you
restore me.

I will seek you because you remove the humanness of my ugly
heart.

You see me for who and what I am, faults and victories,
Successes and failures.

I humbly call upon you and honor you because you love me
when my love toward you wavers and is with condition.

I thank you.

Betrayal

I know that you have betrayed me.
Your eyes tell me of the gravity of your sin that you so
graciously hide beneath a smile.
Betrayal is the mark of a bitter person who confuses self-
worth with self-imposed grandeur.
And so your cycle of betrayal devours your consciousness, and
lies slip out of your lips.
I will not cower, for there is no profit.
I will not hide because all sins are exposed in time.

Betrayal has no recourse.
Betrayal produces no fruit.
Betrayal leaves the pompous glutton full unto vomitus,
flowing out of mouth.
Betrayal leads the strong to weaken under the weight of lies
current and past.

Seek no more to betray.
Seek truth and humbly say, "I will betray no more."
It is then that your soul will be set free.

These Eyes, These Hands

These eyes, these hands.

Open, ready to warm you in life's cold winters.

Eyes sealed shut from prejudice, blind to the pain of anger and betrayal.

Teach me; open your hands, your eyes.

Reach me.

End the loneliness within my soul.

Your eyes, your hands.

Friends Fade

Friends fade like the tears on a weary child's face,
like the mountain that sees the sky age and cry.
Love held the pieces once of bitterness that
had no foundation—yet friends fade.
So I shall wait for time to pass, for I am the weary child.
And mountains shall crumble before me, for I am the sky.
For friends fade, and one day, shall I?
Forgiveness seems the only option.

Judas

There is a Judas that lies deep within us all.
His jewels of hatred form a crown we reap when time
has born a sorrow or joy that we feel to betray.
We utter words of lies and yearnings of disgust,
for all of us have a Judas within us.

A Prayer of Request

I ask, dear God, for little.

May I have this mere return?

My Wants

1. A person with whom to share my dreams, to comfort me in my times of need, and to hold me tenderly forever.

2. I want a million dollars in order to bestow peace in my miserable financial life.

3. I want a child so that my life will be complete.

This, all I ask Lord, and nothing more—thank you.

God's Answer to the Request

My child, how big are your requests!

1. You ask for someone to care for *you* and comfort *you* and hold *you*.

   Love, true love, is unconditional and must be offered beyond yourself to another. If you cannot show love nor live love, it shall never be showered upon you.

2. You ask for money to solve your financial problems; money solves no problems.

   It was money that created your many woes. Why do you whimper over dimes? Money solves nothing that the human heart created. You are best at peace when you give regard to the soul.

3. A child can never properly be cared for by a child. I suggest you allow yourself more time to mature. Remember, my child, vanity holds no value for the carrier of selfishness. The only reward of vanity is profound loneliness and isolation as one seeks to be comforted and reassured of a beauty and intellect that has tenuous longevity.

Parable of the Angel's Short Time

An angel asked a friend of mine if she might have her child.
My friend agreed but for a short time and a small fee.
So the angel agreed and paid the sum. And the child was hers
for a time … a short time.

One day when short time had passed, the woman crouched on
her knees and in prayer asked that the angel might return her
child. The angel appeared to her and said, "In time you shall
see the child, for he awaits you at the borders of time, short
time."

Time passed; the woman aged and soon died of a bitter heart
for the child she never saw.
On her death, her soul did rise to an awaiting Lord.

"Dear woman, where is your child?" asked her Lord.

The woman cried and moaned in agony of regret. "I sold her
to an angel of shadows. Set the angel on fire, Lord, set the
angel on fire; my child was never returned!"

The Lord responded, "You sold your child to an angel? You
paid an evil price. Your flesh and blood did linger at the scent
of money green. Your greed alone is unworthy, your sins a
load to bear … You sold your child for Satan's pleasure."

The woman's soul was swept away and now forever tarries in a lake of fire, of bright, rich fire fed from a green hand. One day the woman saw a child pass her with white and woolen wings. The child called down to the woman, another woman at her side with wings of woolen white, "Momma, time is short, and wisdom begs us to use it wisely."

Lullaby to a Child

Pack your dreams for another day.
Lullaby's go, but dreams stay.
Sleep, my child, sleep.

Papa loves you, and so do I.
Take our love with you, my dear child, to your dreams at
night, for it shall keep you safe.
Sleep, my child, sleep; Papa and I love you.

Johnny

Johnny was a quiet boy who never spoke a word.
For Johnny was beat with an old stick upon each parent's entering.
Mother poured her heart onto Father, but Father would reject her.
So Mother would beat Johnny until her hurt went away, and tears only remained.

Father … he did the same when doubt aroused his curiosity.
So Johnny was a silent boy who never spoke a word, not even as they lowered him into his grave.

Mother and Father, they wept a lot and held blood-stained hands while the townspeople prayed.
After the grave was covered and the dirt was given a cemented piece of Johnny's name, his parents went back home, where the hurt and aroused curiosity continued and death remained.

Grandpa

He couldn't read or write.
He couldn't tell time or drive a car.
But he could feel the sunshine on his face and touch the soil to test it for perfected births.

He could touch a soul, even a heart.
Grandpa could do many things that the modern world could never appreciate for my grandpa was real, and real men last forever.

I love you, Grandpa.

Loneliness

Loneliness, isolation in crowds,
A solemn stare, deep in thought,
Contemplation of faults echoed in one's head of judgment and
condemnation.

Forward thinking lacking,
Successes in question,
Lonely and feeling unloved.

Failures to the lonely are magnified though minute.
Loneliness clouds the mind and pollutes the spirit.
Loneliness is a choice and not a solution.

Face life's realities.
Pain is normative.
Loneliness is an enemy; recognize that you are the victor of
this silent killer.

Destiny

Destiny is her name.
Born from a barren womb,
Prayed for when drugs filled a mother's veins.

Tears of an infant in pain,
Choices of a mother now filled with shame.
But Destiny survives.

Calls upon the lives of others often begin in shame.
Difficulties compromise our beginnings but have no effect on
our endings.
Destiny is her name.

Broken

Questioning my very being,
Believing what others say I am.
Insecure.

Broken.

Not able to see beyond my own mistakes,
Punishing of my own thoughts and opinions.
Where is my identity?

Broken.

In the mirror, I question my own beauty inside and out.
Doubt surrounds me.

Broken.

Reaching toward a God that I am not certain remembers my
burdens, my hurts.
Or is it merely me, and brokenness is an empty perception.

Sleep

Asleep.
I awake in heaven.
Mourners below I see.

No need to ask why.
Peace I know you've given me.

Tired.
Life, beautiful.
A daughter and husband left behind.
A beloved brother.

God knew I was tired.
Death must have been near.
My focus grew more upon you.

No illness, yet I am here.
No sickness, yet I am here.
Sleeping.

Future

At times, a mother carries the burden of a wayward child
beyond her ability.
The burden needs to be given to one greater than she and her
husband.
A family divided over a sin.

Look to the future.
Sin has no power that can win.

Frustrated, burdened, and sad,
A child wayward will be set free.
A family must pray, and answered prayer will prevail.

A child lost who was introduced to the Lord always comes
home.
This is His promise.
This is what the mother and father must uncompromisingly
believe.

Whispers

Behind closed doors you whisper.
Betrayals and stories of others who have done you no harm.

Righteous, you hide your whispers behind a smile.
There is no good intent.
Just whispers.

When will you learn that whispers will consume you as you
examine truths that have no meaning to you?
Yet, you whisper.

Identity

Loss of identity, like a penny in the sea, tossed and quickly
sinking into the depths of the abyss,
Furlong the search for self.

Identity, loss by a society that denies the gift of individuality.

Lost, lost, search some more.

Found, found, never lost.

Social Justice

Social justice.
Eyes closed, a terminology unlived by most.
Hatred hidden under a demagogue of words and edifices large and expansive.

Do you really feel love for the weaker, the poor, or are they just terms conducive to percentages and data?

Social justice.

Politically correct, no color or language I see.
What truly is revealed is the ignorance inside of me.

Escape

Journey into a confusion that is not my own.
Self-imposed by another.
Escape.

Silent is the noise in my head.
Only I hear the confusion as I internalize the noise.
I must escape.

Fear is a lonely traveler.
The silent noise now echoes in my brain.
Repeat, repeat.

My only option is to make the confusion externally known
And not escape, but stand still, face-to-face victorious.

Heard

I heard that you were unhappy here,
Searching for something new.

I heard that you were afraid that we were abandoning you.
I sought to let you know that you were wrong.
But missed the opportunity to tell you, and now you are gone.

I cannot understand why you wept alone and left.
Did you not know the depth of my love for you?

I tell you in my dreams, the loss and pain I feel.
All because you think I did not hear you.

I Heard.

Invited

Come to the table, overflowing with blessings.
This seat is for you.

Sit with me and talk.
I enjoy listening to all that you say.

I have been waiting for you to answer my invitation.
Welcome, I am glad you finally came.

Gone

Tears trickle down.
In shock.
Can't explain what has happened.

Gone.

Recollection of days before,
Life, breath, presence.
Not gone.

Lonely.
How can I recover?
How can I go on?

Gone.

Seed

Planted in fertile soil, you grew.
Destiny known only by God,
You grew.

Untouched by a human hand, intricate details.
Beyond finite minds, so much unknown.
You grew.

Righteous calm.
Unexpected.
Will you survive?

Born.
Eyes so beautiful, spirit calm.
A seed come to life.

Soul Hunger

Sometimes I open my mouth to share rejection experiences.
My sharing seems to fall on deaf ears.

Perhaps rejection makes others feel uncomfortable, as a
society seeks to unite.
Divided by ignorance tolerated, I seek to connect.
But how much can one take when ignorance does not have a
filter.

My soul hungers at times for peace and absence of judgment.
Yet, I sense in-genuineness and it bothers me.

Perhaps the soul is meant to hunger so it seeks comfort from
its Creator.

I'll pray for you

I didn't know how much you were hurting.
You always seem so angry.

Storms come and suns rise.
Somehow your humanness escaped my own consciousness.
I just did not trust you.

Forgive me.
I will pray for you.

Bloom

Sun shines beneath the large flower petals.

Rain drops, fragile become the petals.

Delicate.

The petals must survive the trauma of wind, rain, and the over exposure of the sun.

Bloom.

Sunlight nurtures the flower and although death approaches and petals wither, the flower survives to bloom again.

Rush

Busyness of the day.

Rush.

The body, an image blurred in speed.

Distortion.

Worry envelopes the mind, facial expressions reveal anxiety.

Rush.

I need to slow down, but when?

Life passes quickly, no need to rush when the hands of a clock will do it for you.

Captive

I'm held captive by my sin.

It devours me.

All because I allow it to.

Captive, alone and isolated.

Sin, a choice I made.

A bitterness that will not allow me to forgive.

I hold myself Captive.

God, forgive me.

Love Blinded

A blinded love is one that loses sensitivity to harm.

Vulnerable.

Lost.

Blaming of others who recognize their blindness, they seek to ignore the absence of true love.

Love blinded, bestowed upon no one, but yet stolen hearts are taken.

Lost.

Vulnerable.

Love blinded.

Unconditional

God, I love you unconditionally.

Sometimes I cannot understand why you love me.

Broken.

Fragile.

Fearful.

All qualities of one of little faith.

Yet, you love me unconditionally.

Thank you God for your mercy and grace.

He

Eyes open wide, he sees her pain.

He loves her.

Vows taken, cancer not the plan-- He weeps.

Too young to die.

Dreams collide with reality.

He looks at her--Beautiful and strong, frail and weak.

Questions his own strength.

Perseveres because he loves her.

He--Stronger than even he himself realizes.

She

She,
Touches a long scar where her breast use to be.
Tears,
She clutches the hand of He.
She knows He loves her no matter the storms life brings.
They---Pray together, holding hands tightly in a grasp.

She and He know they are not alone.

God---He listens to the prayers of He and She.

She, no longer afraid, believes in her healing.
Peace found in her love of He and her belief in God.

Regret

Fret.

Mending, but not yet.

Guilt and Shame.

Wondering what really is my name, my personal viewpoint.

Seeking clarity for a mind confused.

Regret.

So sorry for the choices I have made.

Looking beyond myself and seeking forgiveness.

Rebellion

Not listening to you.
Hate you right now.

Why should I?
Authority means nothing.

Toxic are my thoughts and plans when I rebel against
humanity.

Neighbors

More than a few doors down,
People living life just like you.
People lonely and suffering too.
Just like you.

What if a hand was waved, a smile given?
What if support was given to a stranger?

The irony of the neighbor is that they have the potential in our lives, to become friends.
Yet, in the busyness of life, the neighbor is estranged.

Our greatest gift to be discovered are our neighbors.
Seek to know yours.

Toxicity

Poisoned are the words that proceed out of our mouths.
Cursed thinking devours potentiality.

Lying, prejudice, killing, and hate.
These are the many things the human heart can create.

Beckoned by an empty soul, we toil amongst the worms at days end.
Was the lie so worth your soul's departure?

A rise to fame, a title to obtain.
Insecure, choosing to love no more.

Toxic by our own choosing, death approaches our gates and the toxic mind chooses hate.

Help Me to Accept My Faults

I have many faults.
Much brokenness.
Seldom do I own Perfection.

Humanness warrants that I accept that which is broken,
My Humanity.

I have many faults.
Thoughts of perpetual failure impede thinking.
Progression proceeds only when humanness is exposed.

Embrace your faults.
Embrace your brokenness,
Know that imperfection builds character and makes the weak
strong.

Passion

Solomon's words utter Passion.
Seeking beauty in Wisdom.
Knowing physical beauty will Fade.

Lips of honeysuckle, skin like smooth silk.
Hearts a fire under the Scent of Flesh.

Unconditional is the love felt.
Love beyond eternity.

Passion will fade.
But of unconditional love, there is no end.

Ethnoanatomy- A Woman's Journey

The hands of a woman both delicate and strong,
Capable of writing signatures with a quill, pen or brush
stroke, yet able to lift a child to the bosom and hold heavy
pots filled with bounty from a field of grains, fruits, or
vegetables.

Pots of water carried from remote streams and wells so that
her family may drink.
She is amazing, but even she is unaware of her own beauty and
strength.
The eyes of the woman, deep set, lightening in brightness
as she examines the man she loves, her children, family, and
close friends.
Eyes dimmed through pain, suffering, and hunger.
The woman cries and the eyes fill with tears as her soul
mourns losses in silence.
Sometimes she suffers alone, amidst joy, but the woman
chooses to keep others happy.

This is her calling and this is the woman's journey.

Identity

Searching for me, the me I use to be.
Torn and confused by the enemy.
I gasp, blinded by a new society.

Who am I?
This identity cannot own me.

Yearning for clarity.
They cannot understand my pain.

Or do they?

Much easier to claim the hate, when love is present.
Much easier to search for unacceptance when I want my way.

Do I love me?
Not more than they love me.
I believe I have found my true identity.

Thank you Father---Amen.

Found

Searching for the truth,

My destiny in question.
Feeling isolated in my own tortured mind.

Who loves me the way you do Lord?

Bound by the limitations of my finite mind, I call out to you.
Heal me of my pain, help me become anew.

Find me in my horrid mess.
Cleanse me of my unrighteousness.

Lift this heaviness I feel.
Find me Lord, for I am ill.

Heal my mind, my body, my soul.
Help me Lord, to be broken no more.

I am Found.

Shadows

Climbing the walls, dark shadows I see.
This is not good, Satan this could be.

Shadows go by an empty room.
Demonic possession could not be real, yet souls desperate run away from shadows.

Shadows mock the night.
Shadows hide in the daylight.

God sees the shadows, and his people pompous and without fear.
Yet shadows are explored by many who do not believe in the existence of daylight.

Shadows are the coward's ploy to confuse a people lost among shadows.
God has ended the shadows rein and the soul can rest.

Family Reunion

Can't believe death has come again.
A family harmed by life's inevitable.

Death.

Holidays not the same.
Memories streamed with tears and sorrow.

I wait and have solace.
One day in Heaven we'll have a family reunion.